HOLDING SPACE PRACTICE

FOR SILENT, SECRET SUFFERERS

HOW TO FIND DEEP AND PERMANENT PEACE, HAPPINESS AND INTERNAL JOY REGARDLESS OF PAST TRAUMAS, PRESENT CHALLENGES, OR FUTURE FEARS.

Volume 1, 1st Edition

By

CAROL WEBSTER

Founder of

PRINCIPLE BASED LEARNING

DISCLAIMER

DEDICATION:

ESPECIALLY FOR THOSE WHO SECRETLY AND SILENTLY SUFFER AND ARE NOW WILLING TO FIND DEEP, INTERNAL PEACE AND JOY BY WRITING IN THIS WORKBOOK (even when it may not make sense or you don't feel like it) AS YOU TRUST AND FOLLOW THE PROMPTS IN THIS PRACTICE AND THE WHISPERINGS OF YOUR HEART.

THE HOLDING SPACE PRACTICE *Workbook*

WHAT OTHERS SAY ABOUT
THE HOLDING SPACE PRACTICE

"The Holding Space model has been a paradigm-shifting tool for my life. It helps me step aside from my anxieties and natural tendencies towards judgement of self and other, and instead empowers me to embrace what is. It re-centers me, and reminds me to connect from my heart to myself and others. The Holding Space Practice gives me permission to feel my feelings, without shaming or rejecting parts of my emotional life, but rather seeing all emotions as valid, that deserve their own space. Emotions can be helpful information, even if they are not pleasant. The tool of "Gently Noticing with Curiosity" helps me remember to be still, see what is, and withhold judgment. 'Staying in the Space without Distraction' has become a mantra for me, in this fast-paced modern world that can impede connection with others and even the very experience of our being in our own life. The Holding Space Practice draws upon the best principles of the mindfulness wisdom traditions and provides tools that are easily understandable and applied in everyday life." –**Rachel Sargent**

"Since learning the Holding Space Practice, I feel that I am noticing the beauty in people and places that has always been there but I had been too rushed to see."
–**Betty Hathhorn**

"The holding space model is one of those things that once you hear it, it's as if you've known it all along, like it's been a part of you, something that you can't unlearn, you become it. Holding space for myself and allowing others the space to hold themselves has been freeing. So many stigmas and frustrations have disappeared due to this personal practice. I can see others and accept them as they are without wanting them to change for me. Holding space has had a particular impact on my parenting practice. When I allow myself to take care of me and apply the principles learned within these pages I am a much more calm and accepting parent, friend and spouse." –**Ashley Blackwell**

"When I began learning the Holding Space Practice I was in a very dark place in my life. The tools that I learned helped me overcome struggles and challenges and led me back into the light. I have left them close to my bed to go through them again and again because it's not like I'm done yet." –**Nikki McCann**

"As we travel though life it seems that our Pearl, our essence, becomes clouded, covered over, even scratched and dented and we lose sight of who we really are. The Holding Space Practice has helped me uncover my Pearl of Great Price. This Practice helps me heal and once again, my Beautiful Lustrous Pearl, my essence, is able to SHINE. Sometimes it is easy to work through the content, sometime not...but it has been a Gift and I am grateful to and for "Holding Space" as it brings forth the truth, the essence of who I am, my Pearl, my Pearl of Great Price." –**Teena Burke**

TABLE OF CONTENTS:

FORWARD:

"Wow! After reading Carol's Book, "The Holding Space Practice", I am moved and inspired. She has simply and clearly exposed all the human struggles that keep us hostage to limiting self-perceptions. More importantly, she has made accessible a gentle path towards healing and restoration. By courageously sharing her own story of struggle to find deep peace and joy, she has created a simple yet powerful guide for others to follow. I began the process of reflecting, opening, and seeing pathways that could lead to greater insight and change. This helped me not only to overcome any denial that I might be holding, but normalized my experience. We all could benefit greatly from doing this work of opening to ourselves as well as Holding Space for those whom we love. I look forward to integrating her wisdom into my own experience of healing and growth."

Lani Peterson
Psy. D, Psycologist,
Executive Coach, and Story Expert

INTRODUCTION:

This book is a companion to the "Holding Space Practice" book. Honestly, you do not need this book. All the questions and exercises found in this workbook are the same as the ones found in the text of the Holding Space Practice book. You could get an empty notebook to write down the answers to the questions posed. You could use a personal journal that you keep and write your answers to the questions. You could write the answers on a paper napkin, but I'm not recommending that. ☺

This workbook is published as a convenient place to do your Holding Space Practice.

Advantages for using this workbook include:

- You don't have to re-write questions to give context to your answers as you write. The questions are written in the same order here as you find them in the Holding Space Practice book. You just open to the corresponding page and start writing in the space provided.
- You may want to do the exercises more than one time. Once you go through the practice from beginning to end you get a big picture of how the Holding Space tools fit together. Going back to the beginning after completing it will be a surprisingly different experience When you repeat the process a second (and third and more) time through, you can see your growth when you go back and read earlier responses. Going back to earlier responses helps you remember what it was like at first for you and helps you be patient and compassionate with others who may be going through the practice for their first time.
- This workbook is the same size as the Holding Space Practice book and fits nicely in your bag or drawer or shelf or your hand.
- If you are doing the Holding Space Practice in a group it is easy for everyone to turn to the same page number to find responses as you discuss.

Whether you use this workbook or some other paper, the important thing is that you actually DO the work. Read with the intent to apply the tools. Physically write down your thoughts as instructed. Doodle draw and create your project ideas. Close your eyes and breathe. Share what you learn with someone you trust. In a word RECEIVE deeply and you will find consistent and permanent peace.

Here are the four different levels of receiving:

1. Read. If you choose to benefit from *The Holding Space Practice*, you will need to actually read the material. Obviously, without reading the content you won't get anything out of it. That would be like someone handing you a wrapped present and deciding you don't have time or desire to open it.

2. Think. There are different levels and purposes of reading. For example, you can scan quickly, read something out loud in your best broadcaster's voice to impress someone, read something to check it off your "to do" list. You can read for entertainment, and you can read for information. There is a way to read for deep understanding that takes more time and intention than the previous examples. It may mean reading a phrase or a paragraph and wondering if you really understood it then stopping to think about it. It could mean reading some or all of it more than once. The content is not long, but it is dense. For most people, they need at least a month or more to process the ideas found with each tool as they ponder and think about them.

3. Do. There are some built-in helps to begin to apply *The Holding Space Tools*. One thing you will need is a NOTEBOOK or JOURNAL to write in. Having a consistent place to write answers to questions and exercises will keep your work in one place and, if it is like some of my notebooks I have kept while doing this work, these books become treasures that I go back to as I continue to move ahead. Some things I have written or drawn seemed ordinary when I did them and then later on I have gone back and realized they were more significant than I thought at first.

To really process this work deeply, I give you an assignment to create some kind of art piece that incorporates *The Holding Space Model* in a visual way. This is something you might display in an area where you spend a lot of time.

Your goal is focused on creating something that will help you to remember, internalize and apply what you learn in this book. It can be generated in whatever media: computer, paint, marker, colored pencil, fabric, pottery, up cycling...whatever you feel drawn to use and create.

Here are two examples:

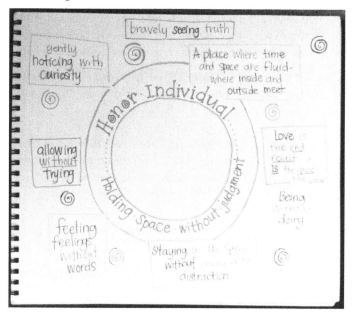

This is a doodle I did. I did not know when I drew this that it would create a significant and positive shift in my life.

I felt compelled to create a large wall hanging to help me remember and internalize *The Holding Space Model* or *Philosophy*. It measures about 4 feet square and hangs in our family room right by my computer where I write.

Others who have done *The Holding Space Workshop* have created a variety of things and sent me photos. You will find your own materials and way of doing this.

> *"Art brings things to light. It illuminates things. It sheds light on our lingering darkness. It casts a beam into the heart of our own darkness and says, See?"*
> Julia Cameron, Artist's Way p.67

4. Share. You can choose anyone you want to share your experiences, insights and questions with. The original workshop was with a small circle of friends.

You may have someone that wants to learn and apply the tools of the *Holding Space Practice* at the same time you are doing it. If so, great! Email them a link to http://www.principlebasedlearning.com/holdingspace/ (or have them buy the book) and invite them to join you. Or maybe you have a good friend who is not doing the practice but is a good listener that you can report to.

It is totally optional, but I encourage you to sign up for a mentor who lives the Holding Space Practice that can answer your questions and be a sounding board. Email carol@principlebasedlearning.com and request a mentor!

The practice of *Holding Space* has everything to do with being willing to freely receive.

C.S. Lewis wrote, *"You must have a capacity to receive, or even omnipotence can't give"*. We think it is easy to receive, but the truth is, it is a practice to make my "personal container bigger" in order to receive more and more.

> *We decide how powerful God is for us. We unconsciously set a limit on how much God can give us or help us. We are stingy with ourselves. And if we receive a gift beyond our imagining, we often send it back!*
> Julia Cameron, Artist Way p. 91

The back side of the metaphorical "receiving coin" is the practice of freely giving. First is the practice of giving thanks. If the only thing you ever apply from *Holding Space* is a gratitude practice, you will find a change in you that defies the simplicity of that practice.

Brené Brown insightfully states: "There is a difference between *feeling* gratitude and *practicing* gratitude. It is during our dark times when we don't *feel* gratitude that *practicing* it makes a difference." It is so true! Gratitude is the key to lasting peace despite any difficult circumstances in life.

I have been trying to live the principle of freely giving and freely receiving. That is why I decided to publish this work as a free gift online to anyone that chooses to receive it along with publishing it paper format. (Some people have told me that work best with paper.) Part of the practice for me is to trust that I will have enough time, energy and resources to continue to spend time helping people with this work. I want it to be available for anyone who needs it. Some would say, "Carol, people will take advantage of your generosity" and I respond, "I hope so!"

GETTING STARTED:

FIRST WRITING ASSIGNMENT:

1. Write down one or more personal challenges in your life that you need to *Hold Space* for yourself. (It may be a personal weakness, bad habit you are trying to overcome, good habit you are struggling to establish, a hard situation you are caught in etc.)

_____

_____

_____

_____

_____

_____

_____

_____

_____

_____

_____

_____

_____

_____

_____

_____

_____

_____

2. Name one person who currently needs space in your life and why. (It might be a family member, co-worker, boss, friend etc.)

_____

_____

_____

_____

_____

_____

_____

_____

_____

_____

_____

_____

_____

_____

_____

_____

_____

_____

_____

_____

_____

_____

_____

You don't need to share these, but it will help you to have real examples in mind as we discuss how to *Hold Space*.

You may want to maintain a written running list as things continue to come up in your life. This practice will help you pause and evaluate which principles best applies in various situations.

Hint: whenever you feel upset, there is something or someone that needs space.

Once you have completed this writing assignment, continue to *Module 1: BEing Without Doing.*

Additional notes:

MODULE 1:

BEING WITHOUT DOING

All of *The Holding Space Tools* work together. There is not a rank or order of use to the tools, but "being without doing" may be a prerequisite for other tools from the stand point of making time to even begin.

WRITING ASSIGNMENT:

Add to your journal... as you gain insights, share them with someone.

1. Make a list of all the things you do or feel that you should do.

2. Put a star next to the things that you *like* to do.

Put an "X" next to the things you could let go of doing. Think carefully. We often have activities that we think we "have to do", but on further consideration, we really don't have to vacuum or dust every day or cook 3 meals a day or work an extra part time job. It is just what we have come to believe. In truth we could make changes in what we value or think we should value and let go of activities that crowd our life.

CENTERING EXERCISE:

1. Arrange a time when you are alone and won't be disturbed. I know that sounds totally impossible for some, especially for mothers of young children. Don't worry. You will figure it out sooner or later. Once you hit "bottom" you become ill enough that you end up in bed. Illness is a well-disguised blessing. You will eventually find a way to proactively create that quiet alone time without having to be sick to get it if you want to keep working at centering.

2. In that quiet space get comfortable. I usually do that lying down with a blanket and pillow to make me comfortable. I have also done this reclined in a car waiting for a child in his/her class or activity. I do this at the end of exercise (yoga) and now can do it in a variety of situations...but that was after a lot of practice and is not as effective as a set-aside time. So get quiet and comfortable.

3. Now, just notice. Don't try to DO or change anything. Just notice. Your brain might be racing. That is ok. You might notice something that hurts. That's ok. You might drop off to sleep. No problem. You might cry, giggle, feel frustration, think this is a dumb waste of time, feel antsy, feel peaceful or ANYTHING. It is all ok. Just notice. There is no wrong way to do this other than not doing it at all.

Record your experience with this centering exercise. Repeat at least 3 different days and notices how your experience differs.

Day 1:

Day 2:

Day 3:

Additional notes:

MODULE 2:
BRAVELY SEEING TRUTH

- *It takes courage to decide to look more deeply at a pattern that feels "normal" and comfortable.*

- *It takes courage to admit that what I thought was right, or what my parents taught me was right (either verbally or by example), is actually not the truth.*

- *It takes courage to unlock and change these erroneous patterns once I see the error because it will likely evoke strong feelings both inside of me and possibly inside the people around me who might feel uncomfortable with changes I make.*

WRITING ASSIGNMENT:

Add to your journal… as you gain insights, share them with someone.

1. Describe a specific situation where "bravely seeing truth" was needed in your life.

2. Describe how you felt when you discover something you *thought* was true ended up being false.

_____

_____

_____

_____

_____

_____

_____

_____

_____

_____

_____

_____

_____

_____

_____

_____

_____

_____

_____

_____

_____

_____

_____

_____

Shame is painful for

children

because it is linked to the **fear** of being **unloveable**.

→

Must learn to:
cope, manage, manipulate
hide, survive, pretend,
go away, please, fight
rebel, act out,
be strong-willed

young children

are dependent on parents
for **survival**.

Feeling unloveable is a
threat to survival.

→

They feel and react:
utterly vunerable
powerless
easy to bully
won't tell or can't tell
can be manipulated

-It's trauma-

We revert to feeling

childlike

and small

when adult shame experiences
trigger early childhood **traumas**.

→

Adult reactions:
acting childish
throwing fits
pouting and whining
bury emotions
run away
change the subject
live from coping mask
don't cry
"fake it 'til you make it"

paraphrasing Brené Brown
"Daring Greatly" page 225

What are ways you see yourself in this chart?

_____

_____

_____

_____

_____

_____

_____

_____

_____

_____

CENTERING EXERCISE:

---

1. Think of a time recently that you criticized someone. You may or may not have said anything out loud. Can you see how the thing you saw "wrong" in someone else may be a weakness you don't like about yourself? Whatever we notice in others is ALWAY a reflection of our self. The thing that bothers us most in others is the thing that bothers us most about ourselves, but usually I don't want to see it, so I become blind to it.

Describe this situation:

_____

_____

_____

_____

_____

_____

_____

_____

_____

_____

_____

_____

_____

_____

_____

_____

_____

_____

---

3. **Look through some childhood photos of yourself.** (Or simply think back
   if photos are not accessible.) What was an age when you felt sad, angry,
   discouraged or challenged? Imagine meeting that younger "you".
   Knowing what you know now, what would you say to encourage and/or
   comfort that child? Speak or write to him/her as a loving and wise parent
   and record it in your journal.

Seeing the truth can be very difficult *during* the process. You can lose center (who am I?) and feel ungrounded (where am I in relationship to people and things around me?).

Try this: Sit in a quiet place. Begin by exhaling all your air out then slowly take in an inhale, count that as breath one.

Exhale and inhale = breath two. Continue the exhale and inhale breath to 9. If you focus on this exercise you will find a sense of calm and center by the time you get to the 9th breath. It is common for the thoughts to wander before you get to the 9th breath. No big deal. Just notice that and bring your thought back to your breath and begin to count again: exhale, inhale= breath one. This is not a counting exercise; it is a way to notice your thoughts and gently bring them into focus. It is a practice, not a competition or judgment.

What do you do to feel grounded or "down to earth?" You may already have a practice that works well. If so, be sure to continue it and add the "exhale/inhale" exercise.

_____

_____

_____

_____

_____

_____

_____

_____

_____

_____

_____

_____

_____

_____

3. Stand somewhere quietly. Imagine you are a tree and your feet have roots growing down into the ground. Exhale and imagine the breath going down your body and legs and out to those imaginary roots. As you begin to inhale, "see" the breath gathering energy and nutrition from the earth and up into your body.

Retain your breath as the energy swirls then let the exhale glide down your body, legs, feet and out to the "roots" then bring the breath back up the pathway. Repeat this 3-9 times. This exercise helps you feel grounded.

Record your experience with this centering exercise. Repeat at least 3 different days and notices how your experience differs.

Day 1:

_____

_____

_____

_____

_____

_____

_____

_____

_____

_____

_____

_____

_____

_____

_____

_____

Day 2:

_____

_____

_____

_____

_____

_____

_____

_____

_____

_____

_____

_____

_____

_____

_____

_____

_____

_____

_____

_____

_____

_____

_____

_____

__Day 3:__

Additional notes:

Additional notes:

_____

_____

_____

_____

_____

_____

_____

_____

_____

_____

_____

_____

_____

_____

_____

_____

_____

_____

_____

_____

_____

_____

_____

_____

_____

MODULE 3:
FEELING FEELINGS WITHOUT WORDS

How can I tell if I am happy? Sad? Angry? Afraid? We have words for those feelings, but the feelings are not those words. If I pay attention, I can locate some sensation in my body associated with these feelings. For example, if I try to hold back tears there is a pressure in my throat (a "lump in my throat"). When anger arises I clench my jaw and my fists and my arms tighten. When I am nervous or scared I feel queasiness or "butterflies" in my stomach. Sometimes I feel a deep sadness up and down the center core of my body. Excitement can send a zingy, moving sensation and love a warm, glowing feeling in my chest.

WRITING ASSIGNMENT:

Add to your journal... as you gain insights, share them with <u>someone</u>.

1. Identify at least 4 emotions and where you feel those feelings in your body.

_____

_____

_____

_____

_____

_____

_____

_____

_____

_____

_____

_____

2. Describe one specific example in your life when you felt emotional overwhelm.

Nurture the mindset that all feelings are valid and useful, and learn to allow our feelings to rise and process.

CENTERING EXERCISE:

Different people deal with feelings in different ways. Rate yourself on a scale from 1-5 for the following with 1 being "very likely" and a 5 being "very unlikely":

- When I feel sad I try to never cry in public
- When I feel excited I jump, giggle, laugh, whoop etc.
- When I feel frustrated I grit my teeth
- When I feel ticked-off I get really quiet
- When I feel disappointed I pretend like I don't care
- When someone else yells at me I yell right back at them
- When I see a beautiful sunset I take a photograph
- When a child says something cute I smile
- When I watch movies I often cry
- When I hear something funny I laugh out loud
- When I text LOL it is because I really have LOLed

There is no right or wrong way to display emotions, but it is important to notice how you react and notice if the ways you display feelings serve you well or not.

Write about one emotion or situation where your tendency toward an emotion is not useful.

_____

_____

_____

_____

_____

Art Project: Part of the *Holding Space Practice* is to create some piece of original art work using *The Holding Space Model.*

Create YOUR art of *The Holding Space Chart.* Your project is to help you to remember, internalize and apply the *Holding Space tools.* It can be generated in whatever media: paper or canvas with, paint, marker, and colored pencil, fabric with embroider, quilting, pottery, up cycling, computer graphics, whatever you feel drawn to use and create. I look at my *Holding Space* art every day when I am in our family room. It helps me every day.

Being creative uses a different part of the brain than reading, writing and talking. That is why part of the practice is to create something with your hands. *The Holding Space Model* is not something to theorize about… it is something to experience.

If you think, "I'm not creative. She is only talking about people that do art." Then you need to do this more than anyone! It is NOT the end product but the process of doing it that matters. If you don't want to show it to anyone, that is your choice, but make time to experience learning through creating!

Write here and share with a friend or your mentor what medium you think you will use and any other thoughts on your art work assignment. That will help you to have energy to move forward. Maybe you have already started. Let your friend or mentor know that.

Maybe you have some really good excuse why you can't/won't do this. You might find out something about yourself if you share that thought. If you are thinking, "I don't have enough time. I'm too busy" then think about why that is the case. If you are thinking, "That is dumb. It feels like an elementary school homework assignment and I'm and adult!" then think about why you think that. Maybe you feel anxiety over this. Notice, don't judge. Start where you are and move forward.

Sketch or doodle ideas for your Holding Space project

Sketch or doodle ideas for your Holding Space project

Sketch or doodle ideas for your Holding Space project

MODULE 4:
ALLOWING WITHOUT TRYING

What is it about trying "too hard" that somehow morphs from appropriate determination to something problematic?

Allowing without trying (too hard, too much) means letting go of judging myself and others.

Holding Space means allowing myself and others to be who we are; to accept and appreciate our gifts and strengths as well as to accept individual weakness and "works in progress".

WRITING ASSIGNMENT:

Add to your journal… as you gain insights, share them with someone.

1. Who do you know that tries too hard? What is it like to be around them?

_____

_____

_____

_____

_____

_____

_____

_____

_____

_____

_____

_____

_____

_____

2. Describe one example of a time you tried too hard in the past or
    something you recognize you are doing currently. In other words, is
    there something you are trying to control?

_____

_____

_____

_____

_____

_____

_____

_____

_____

_____

_____

_____

_____

_____

_____

_____

_____

_____

_____

_____

_____

_____

_____

3. Identify a time you have judged someone harshly. Is the thing you were criticizing something that, if you can be really honest with yourself, you realize that you too struggle with?

_____

_____

_____

_____

_____

_____

_____

_____

_____

_____

_____

_____

_____

_____

_____

_____

_____

_____

_____

_____

_____

_____

Allowing without trying is the key to peaceful success.
I did not say it is the key to success; I said
it is the key to <u>peaceful</u> success.

WRITING ASSIGNMENT:

Add to your journal… as you gain insights, share them with someone.

1. Define what "success" is for you.

_____

_____

_____

_____

_____

_____

_____

_____

_____

_____

_____

_____

_____

_____

_____

2. What is peace?

_____

_____

_____

_____

_____

_____

_____

_____

_____

_____

_____

_____

_____

_____

_____

_____

_____

_____

_____

_____

_____

_____

_____

_____

3. Is *peaceful* success different from your definition of "success" above?

Additional notes:

Additional notes:

Additional notes:

MODULE 5:
GENTLY NOTICING WITH CURIOSITY

Somewhere along the way most of us loose the gift of curiosity that we had as children.

Part of *Holding Space* is to develop (re-develop actually) the mindset of gentle curiosity. This is the gateway to mindfulness. It is the ability to drop assumptions that we already "know" something and be able to, in a child-like way, see things as a first time learner. But how do I do that?

Before we can rediscover curiosity we need to explore how we lost it in the first place.

Do you remember as a child making an honest mistake and "getting in trouble" for it?

Have you ever reacted to a child who has been:

- Too loud?
- Too slow?
- Too hyper?
- Too whiny?
- Too excited?
- Too ... fill-in-the-blank

What would happen if, instead of resisting, I bravely embrace my "wrongness"?

WRITING ASSIGNMENT:

Add to your journal… as you gain insights, share them with <u>someone</u>.

Think about *all* of these questions, but *write out* your answer to at least two of them.

1. How does a person learn to gently notice with curiosity?

_____

_____

_____

_____

_____

_____

_____

_____

_____

_____

_____

_____

_____

_____

_____

_____

_____

_____

_____

2. How does a person go about observing their own thoughts and feelings and reactions? and How does a person make sense and use of their observations?

_____

_____

_____

_____

_____

_____

_____

_____

_____

_____

_____

_____

_____

_____

_____

_____

_____

_____

_____

_____

_____

3. Do you consider yourself a good observer? Why or why not?

4. Which of the senses do you find particularly sensitive for you? (Sight, sound, taste, smell, tactile, internal feeling... Other?) What is it like? When has your special sensitivity been helpful and when has it been hard?

_____

_____

_____

_____

_____

_____

_____

_____

_____

_____

_____

_____

_____

_____

_____

_____

_____

_____

_____

_____

_____

_____

_____

_____

CENTERING EXERCISE:

Part I: If you are following along, you already have paper and pen in hand. Stop. Listen for 30 seconds or so. Next pick up your pen and write down what you noticed hearing. Stop and listen again for 1-2 minutes. (Longer if you like). Write down anything else you heard that may not have been present in the first 30 seconds or that was there but you had not noticed at first.

Part II: Do the same thing observing what you can hear for at least 1-2 minutes, but add to your observing anything you feel. Are you cold/hot? Can you feel fabric touching you? Is there a tight muscle anywhere? What is your posture like? Any other sensations? Just observe. Stop and write. Observe again. Write again.

_____

_____

_____

_____

_____

_____

_____

_____

_____

_____

_____

_____

_____

_____

_____

_____

_____

_____

_____

_____

_____

_____

Part III: *You may want to do part III right now or after a break or later today or tomorrow. Put your mind back into observing mode. Close your eyes this time (maybe you naturally closed your eyes on part I and part II.., something to gently notice).*

Lay down this time (maybe you naturally laid down on part I and part II... something else to gently notice... No judgment. There is no right or wrong.) In this quiet, reclined, eye-closed position, notice your thoughts for at least one minute. If you find it difficult to notice your thoughts, simply notice your breathing. Don't try to change your breathing, just notice when you inhale and exhale. Try to count each breath cycle counting your exhale as 1. In and out is 2 until you get to 10 then start over again at one. Somewhere along the way you will discover that you went from counting to a thought. What is the thought?

When you feel ready, open your eyes and write the thoughts that came to you. You may find thoughts flowing even as you write. Don't judge if these thoughts are good or bad, right or wrong.

Don't try to change your thoughts, just observe them. Begin to write them as fast as you can unworried about penmanship or legibility, grammar or spelling. Write for at least a page and, preferably, for three pages (but no more in one sitting). Do NOT go back and read what you wrote. *What* your thoughts were is *not* the exercise. Practicing observing your thoughts without judging them is the point.

_____

_____

_____

_____

_____

_____

_____

_____

_____

_____

_____

_____

_____

_____

_____

_____

_____

_____

_____

_____

_____

_____

_____

_____

_____

_____

_____

_____

**There is little growth in your comfort zone.
and there is little comfort in your growth zone.**

Increase your growth zone by noticing where it is and extending your tolerance of staying in it. This brings us full circle back to *Holding Space* for self.

Additional notes:

_____

_____

_____

_____

_____

_____

_____

_____

_____

_____

_____

_____

_____

_____

_____

_____

_____

_____

_____

_____

_____

_____

_____

_____

_____

_____

MODULE 6:
STAYING IN THE SPACE WITHOUT GIVING IN TO DISTRACTION

When we begin to be mindful, to bravely look for truth, to gently observe and feel feelings there is a normal pull toward distraction.

Tempting distractions include:

- Sleep
- Reading
- Analytical thinking
- Getting busy (cleaning the house, going to my "to do" list)
- Writing this
- Picking a fight
- Check email/text
- Turn on a show (TV, Browse internet, you tube, music, sports)
- Eat, cook
- Fix someone else
- Talk to someone
- Planning
- Fantasizing
- Other _____

Notice the distraction and gently return to your breath and feel the sensation

Examples of "staying in the space" include:

- Meditation
- Pondering
- Sincere prayer
- Conscious breathing
- Self-calming
- Centering
- Grounding...

What other ideas or phrases help you *Hold Space*?

_____

_____

_____

_____

_____

_____

_____

_____

_____

_____

_____

_____

_____

_____

_____

_____

_____

_____

_____

_____

_____

_____

_____

WRITING ASSIGNMENT:

Add to your journal… as you gain insights, share them with <u>someone</u>.

1. Are you becoming more aware of the voice inside your head? What is it like? What are examples of things it says?

_____

_____

_____

_____

_____

_____

_____

_____

_____

_____

_____

_____

_____

_____

_____

_____

_____

_____

_____

_____

2. Do you catch yourself getting caught up in old conditioned responses? Other ways to ask this question is: Do you recognize times when you are caught in a mental loop or holding grudges or stuck in a useless pattern that keep repeating itself? Can you recognize self-critical thoughts? If so, write 2-3 examples.

3. Write 3 or more ways that you "numb" or "resist what is".

_____

_____

_____

_____

_____

_____

_____

_____

_____

_____

_____

_____

_____

_____

_____

_____

_____

_____

_____

_____

_____

_____

_____

_____

4. Write 4 or more things that make you feel loved and accepted.

Physical Exercise: An essential part of doing this work is appropriate physical exercise and nutrition. Simply stated, it takes energy and we get our energy from a combination of food and movement. The Chinese call this energy qi (chi) and yoga calls it *prana*.

Here are some questions to answer in your journal:

1. What are you doing for exercise?

_____

_____

_____

_____

_____

_____

_____

_____

_____

_____

_____

_____

_____

_____

_____

_____

_____

_____

_____

_____

2. What gentle shifts do you need to increase your body awareness?

3. What gentle shifts will help you begin or maintain consistent exercise in your life?

_____

_____

_____

_____

_____

_____

_____

_____

_____

_____

_____

_____

_____

_____

_____

_____

_____

_____

_____

_____

_____

_____

4. What has worked for you before, or is currently working well?

5. What exercise would you like to try that you haven't? What stops you from trying it?

_____

_____

_____

_____

_____

_____

_____

_____

_____

_____

_____

_____

_____

_____

_____

_____

_____

_____

_____

_____

_____

_____

_____

6. What hurts in your body that needs attention? Where can you research something that could be helpful to you? (Typical answers include low back, shoulders, neck, headaches, knees, hips...)

_____

_____

_____

_____

_____

_____

_____

_____

_____

_____

_____

_____

_____

_____

_____

_____

_____

_____

_____

_____

_____

_____

7. If you knew that sticking with your exercise would give what you need to help someone who is suffering, who would you be willing to do that for? (Typical answers include a child/your children, spouse, friend, student….)

Additional notes:

Additional notes:

MODULE 7:
A PLACE WHERE TIME AND SPACE ARE FLUID.
WHERE INSIDE AND OUTSIDE MEET

Holding Space, then, is a place where I can be aware of time and space but also let go of time and space at appropriate times. It is the place where inside (that eternal part of me) and outside (the physical part of me) meet.

This is not a new idea. We all remember the famous **Shakespeare** quote *"To thine own self be true"*.

All of *The Holding Space Tools* lead us to this place.

Meditation is a conscious decision to surrender to an internal place without surrendering to sleep or mind wandering

WRITING ASSIGNMENT:

Add to your journal… as you gain insights, share them with <u>someone</u>.

1. What helps you to go to a relaxed alert state?

_____

_____

_____

_____

_____

_____

_____

_____

_____

_____

_____

_____

_____

_____

_____

_____

_____

_____

_____

_____

_____

_____

_____

2. What will you try to add to a meditation/revelation practice?

_____

_____

_____

_____

_____

_____

_____

_____

_____

_____

_____

_____

_____

_____

_____

_____

_____

_____

_____

_____

_____

Native American cultures believe that an important part of life is to receive a *Sacred Wound*. The idea is that there is some challenge(s) or injury inflicted upon every person that is meant to be a learning opportunity.

Part of the life path is to do what it takes to heal from our wounds.

JOURNAL OR ART ACTIVITY:

Based on some of Brené Brown's exercises (google search her!)

You will need to look for two photos** of yourself for this:

Photo #1: Find a photo of yourself when you were very young...maybe two or three years old. Make a copy of it to glue or tape it into your journal or create an art piece with it. ** (**Photos help, but if none are available to you, don't let that be an excuse to skip this. Use your memory, an object that reminds you of your childhood like a toy, stuffed animal, or even a photo of another child (perhaps your own child or grandchild etc.) The point is to go to a place inside and "meet" yourself there. This is an opportunity to practice letting go of time and space.

Look at the photo of yourself and go back to that time when you were innocent.

Your photo here

#1

From the point of view of your adult self, relate to that younger part of you. At that early age you were authentically you!

It was definitely there when you were two or three. Looking at that photo, answer (and write down) these questions:

- What do you see when you look at her/him?

_____

_____

_____

_____

_____

_____

_____

_____

_____

- What do you love and appreciate about her/him?

_____

_____

_____

_____

_____

_____

_____

_____

_____

_____

_____

_____

- What makes her/his light shine?

_____

_____

_____

_____

_____

_____

_____

_____

_____

_____

- How can you take care of her/him?

_____

_____

_____

_____

_____

_____

_____

_____

_____

_____

_____

2. Photo #2: Find a photo of yourself when you first started worrying about what others think of you (perhaps age 8-12) and maybe had small worries or serious challenges.

Look at the photo of yourself and go back to that time when you were innocent.

Your photo here

#2

From the point of view of your adult self, relate to that younger part of you.

Compassionately "talk" to that younger you. Give her/him advice and comfort that would have really helped you through that time. Write down that advice.

_____

_____

_____

_____

_____

_____

_____

_____

_____

_____

_____

_____

_____

_____

_____

_____

_____

_____

_____

_____

How does this exercise relate to the other *Holding Space Tools*?

1. Being without doing
2. Bravely seeing truth
3. Feeling feelings without words
4. Allowing without trying
5. Gently noticing with curiosity
6. Staying in the space without giving into distraction
7. A place where time and space are fluid; where inside and outside meet.
8. Love is the end result. It IS the space and circle.

Final Art Project

Have you begun or made progress on your art project? Have you decided not to do it? Have you forgotten?

Here's a recap for your art project:

Your goal is focused on creating something that will help you to remember, internalize and apply what you learn in the *Holding Space Practice*. It can be generated in whatever media: paper or canvas with, paint, marker, colored pencil… fabric with embroider, quilting etc..… pottery, up cycling, computer graphics…whatever you feel drawn to use and create.

I look at my *Holding Space* art every day when I am in our family room. It has helped me apply the tools in my everyday life.

Being creative uses a different part of the brain than reading, writing and talking. That is why part of the *Holding Space Practice* is to create something with your hands. *The Holding Space Model* is not something to theorize about… it is something to experience.

If you think, "I'm not creative, this is only for people that do art." Then you need to do this more than anyone! It is NOT the end product but the process of doing it that matters. If you don't want to show it to anyone, that is your choice, but make time to experience the learning through creating!

Describe briefly to a friend or mentor what medium you think you will use and any other thoughts on your art work assignment. Maybe you have already started. Let your mentor know that. Maybe you have some really good excuse why you can't/won't do this. You might find out something about yourself if you share that thought.

If you are thinking, "I don't have enough time. I'm too busy" then think about why that is the case. If you are thinking, "That is dumb. It feels like an elementary school homework assignment and I'm and adult!" then think about why you think that. Maybe you feel anxiety over this. Notice, don't judge. Start where you are and move forward.

Sketch or doodle *more* ideas for your Holding Space project

Sketch or doodle *more* ideas for your Holding Space project

Sketch or doodle *more* ideas for your Holding Space project

Sketch or doodle *more* ideas for your Holding Space project

Sketch or doodle *more* ideas for your Holding Space project

MODULE 8:
LOVE IS THE END RESULT.
IT *IS* THE SPACE AND THE CIRCLE.

Workshop participant, Kim, found this profound poem by **Mpho Tutu** and passed it along to me.

To whom shall I tell my story?

Who will hear my truth?
Who can open the space that my words want to fill?
Who will hold open this space for the words
that tumble out in fast cutting shards?
And the words that stumble hesitantly into the
world unsure if they're welcome.
Can you hold that space open for me?
Can you keep your questions and suggestions and judgements at bay?
Can you wait with me for the truths that stay hidden behind
my sadness my fear my forgetting and my pain?
Can you just hold open a space for me to tell my story?
(https://soundcloud.com/forgiveness-challenge/to-whom-shall-i-tell-my-story)

This final module of *The Holding Space Practice* explores the art of personal story discovery for self as well as helping others on their journeys.

Lani Peterson uses a beautiful analogy of a tree to help us carefully approach our sacred core stories. **We can get stuck in negative and constraining stories we tell ourselves at unconscious levels**. We can get caught in these riptides that seem to take us further and further from the steady ground of our true self.

We can't just go headlong looking for our stuck stories because when we live in them they are not visible to us.

WRITING ASSIGNMENT:

Add to your journal… as you gain insights, share them with <u>someone</u>.

1. Write a list of people that always (or almost always) make you feel good about yourself. For most people this is a rather short list.

   _____

   _____

   _____

   _____

2. Write a list of activities that you love and feel good (but not numb) while you are doing it.

   _____

   _____

   _____

   _____

3. Continue your list to include things like a single memory, books, authors, or places (maybe a specific garden, vacation spot, house, office, room, church, synagogue or temple.) The possibilities are endless!

   _____

   _____

   _____

   _____

   _____

4. Pick one from any of these lists and write the story of how he, she or it came into your life and how this helps you feel rooted or grounded.

There is a "place" where we are home. It is a place where we always want to return. A place associated with family, acceptance, protection, warmth, relief, belonging, relaxing, safety, consistency... What other words do you associate with home? Write them around the house.

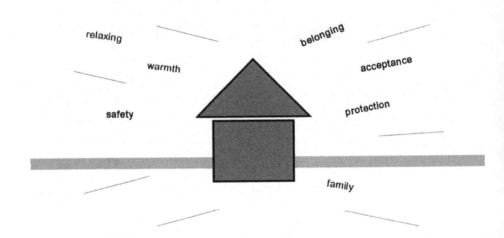

relaxing

belonging

warmth

acceptance

safety

protection

family

WRITING ASSIGNMENT:

Add to your journal… as you gain insights, share them with <u>someone</u>.

• Make a list of words or phrases that you associate with "home"

For those whose childhood home life was less than ideal (and we can ALL think of ways that our childhood was less than ideal!), the word "home" might trigger painful thoughts, feelings or words. The point of exploring your roots is to build a place within you where you belong and can return to whenever you discover you have fallen into a stuck story and feel like the fish yanked out of water or the swimmer stuck in a riptide being pulled out to sea.

This HOME practice stands for:

Honest

Open

Mindful

Energy

If you don't consciously have a place to calm-out when things get tough, the tendency is to run away and/or numb-out which leads us to feel isolated, desperate, ill, and varying degrees of unhappiness or misery.

Once you have begun to establish a HOME practice that you can return to within yourself, then you can move on to writing your own unfolding stories

The practice of *Holding Space*, then, is creating HOME. It is love in the truest sense of that word. It is never-ending like a circle. It IS the circle. This last module is really the first.

Love. Be. Brave. Feel. Allow. Notice. Stay. Flow. Love.

Last assignment: Go back to the beginning and repeat.

Additional notes:

Additional notes:

_____

_____

_____

_____

_____

_____

_____

_____

_____

_____

_____

_____

_____

_____

_____

_____

_____

_____

_____

_____

_____

_____

_____

_____

_____

ACKNOWLEDGEMENTS:

I thank my personal coaches who have dedicated their lives to helping people heal. Each has had a profound and personal influence upon me and taught me step by step, the ideas and concepts found in this book. I was led to each one in miraculous ways. John D. Andre, Frances Blackstock (1931-2015), Michele Kruger, Tisha Mecham, Tung Bui and Kim Johnson with special mention of Kim Meissinger. Nearly all of the core concepts and the vocabulary used to describe the ideas of this book came from conversations in her office and profound email exchanges.

I mention finding these earthly angels miraculously. I know you read people "thank God" in acknowledgment pages, but really, I want to make it very clear that everything I write about in this practice feels like it is not really mine, but God's. The way ideas come into my mind, the way people have shown up on my path has to be influenced beyond by a Being way more intelligent and wise. I call him Father and I humbly thank Him!

The family and people you live with are really the subjects in this experiment we call life. I've been blessed with amazing and patient lab partners: Eric, the #1 love of my life who voluntarily supports me in everything, and our children Kyra, Kallen, Garrett, Travis and Mia. My love for these people is my biggest motivation to practice *Holding Space*. Thank you for your kind patience with an unconventional wife and mother.

To the first *Wisdom Workshop* participants. Those monthly conference calls (and emails) in 2015 motivated me to clothe these ideas in written word. I love you for the lives you are living and the tremendous influence you have on the world. I don't think you understand how spectacular you are. Nikki, Betty, Ashley, Rachel, Teena, Kim, Jackie, Tung. Others couldn't be on the calls in person, but I feel your presence too. Michaela, Kristin, Lori, Jen, Henry, Grit, Neil, Heather, Shawna, Julie, Karin, Annie, Joyce, Lani, Diana and Ed.

Thank you, Ed Murphy, for your encouragement and expertise in transforming the words of this book into a form that makes it widely accessible. Your generosity, gifts, talents, kind patience and tenacity with me are amazing! Any one that reads this book and gets anything out of it can thank Ed for making it a reality.

Lastly, thank YOU, whoever you are, reading this. For some years now Father has given me a "knowing" that there is a circle of people that I am part of. This circle cannot be defined by a political party or church or profession or organization that can be named. This group of people willingly listens to and follows a whispering that can't be explained. You are making a profound difference in the world just by your continual striving to be your best and highest self. The tools of *The Holding Space Practice* are here to help you find deeper and more consistent peace and joy as you make your way through challenges, stress and pain that is part of the intentional growth patterns of this world. Thank you for being the kind of person willing to do "your" work. Dr. Andre used to repeat to me, "See the work. Do the work."

ABOUT THE AUTHOR:

Carol earned her MA and BA degrees in Linguistics at University of Arizona and the University of Utah.

She served a mission in South America, and taught Spanish and Linguistic classes in University to Elementary classrooms. She also participated and led humanitarian projects in Bolivia, Peru and Guatemala.

Because of her *passion* for optimal teaching and learning, she organized *Principle Based Learning (PBL)* to meet the needs of families looking for support in their desire to educate their children which always starts with parents educating themselves first.

As part of that support, she began *Wisdom Workshops* to share healing wisdom that she has gained through years of working with amazing healers to overcome her challenges with fibromyalgia, anxiety and depression.

Carol's brainchild, the *Learning Journey Challenge*, encourages life-long, principle based learning by teaching people how to aim towards building a legacy for coming generations.

She continues to write articles on a variety of topics published on the rich PBL website that she designed and developed.

Carol and her husband Eric homeschool their 5 children and live in Kansas City.

ONE LAST THING...

If you feel this information could help someone else, please take a few moments to let them know. If it turns out to make a difference in their life, they'll be forever grateful to you — as will I.

Let's make a difference together – one person at a time!

All the best!

Carol

Founder of *Principle Based Learning*
email: *Carol@PrincipleBasedLearning.com*

Made in the USA
Monee, IL
16 November 2019